Hands for the Harvest

2002-3 NMI
MISSION EDUCATION RESOURCES

❃ ❃ ❃

READING BOOKS

ADVENTURE WITH GOD
The Jeanine van Beek Story
by Helen Temple

HANDS FOR THE HARVEST
Laborers for the Lord in the Far East
by A. Brent Cobb

JOURNEY TO JERUSALEM
Making a Difference in the Middle East
by Pat Stockett Johnston

MOZAMBIQUE MOMENTS
E-mail from the African Bush
by Douglas J. Perkins and Phyllis H. Perkins

TRIUMPH IN TRINIDAD
God's Promises Never Failed
by Ruth O. Saxon

UNDER THE "L"
Mission Field Chicago
by L. Wayne Hindmand

❃ ❃ ❃

ADULT MISSION EDUCATION RESOURCE BOOK

CALLED TO TEACH
Edited by Wes Eby

Hands for the Harvest

Laborers for the Lord in the Far East

by
A. Brent Cobb

N℗H

Nazarene Publishing House
Kansas City, Missouri

Dedication

To Stephen Brent Cobb,
tender transplanted "seedling"
whose simple faith in his Father God
continues bearing fruit for eternity

Contents

A. Brent Cobb has served as the director of the Asia-Pacific Region for the Church of the Nazarene since 1994. He directs the work of the denomination across a vast area that is home to 40 percent of the world's population. The Church of the Nazarene is now established or registered in 25 world areas on the region with 50 districts, 11 colleges, 1 university, and 1 seminary.

Dr. Cobb and his wife, Marty, served as missionaries in Korea for 10 years from 1970 to 1980. During his first term, he was director of Korean Nazarene Theological College (now Korea Nazarene University). During his second term, he was mission director.

The Cobbs served in several pastorates in the United States, including Seattle First, Sacramento First, and Dallas Bruton Terrace. He also directed both the Asian ministries of Long Beach First Church and Asian Nazarene Bible College Extension in Long Beach.

A graduate of Asbury College and Nazarene Theological Seminary, Brent earned the doctor of ministry degree from Northwest Graduate School in Seattle in 1995. He and Marty have three children: Skyler, Sara, and Adam.

Brent is the author of three previous NMI (formerly NWMS) reading books: *Tried and Triumphant,* 1984-85; *Hasten the Harvest,* 1988-89; and *Furloughs, Furlongs, and Potluck Dinners,* 1995-96.

Acknowledgments

- To the Lord of the eternal harvest who implanted good seeds in my mind and heart more than 50 years ago, I give thanks for His great grace.
- To my godly parents and other spiritual guides, I owe more than I can ever repay.
- To Marty, my wife and finest friend for more than 35 years, I say thanks for being the single most significant human means of grace in my life. Particularly, I'm grateful for her encouragement to me as I attempt to capture people's stories and write them well.
- To five of the six "harvest hands" whose stories are told in these pages, I am grateful for their openness in working with me.
- To Larry West who provided the raw content for Stephen's story, I say thank you.
- To Wes Eby, the creative, compassionate editor for this writing effort, who has taught me much, I am grateful.

The six people's stories themselves have challenged and heartened me. May Jesus Christ be praised.

—Brent Cobb

Introduction

Harvest may come from land, sea, stream, tree, and deep beneath the earth's surface. Fishers with their nets sometimes call their huge hauls "harvests of the sea." Spiritual harvest happens because individuals invest heavily in others. Preparing for an envisioned harvest requires time-consuming, back-breaking work. But the *human harvest* is worth the investment of tears, toil, time, and trust.

Harvest—fruit, vegetables, nuts, grain, fish, diamonds, pearls, and more—is gathered for humanity. The greatest harvest by far is *people*—men, women, youth, and children—gleaned for God.

A true story by an unknown author tells about David Morse, a missionary to India, who became a friend of the pearl diver Rambhau.* David spent many evenings in Rambhau's cabin reading the Bible and explaining to him God's way of salvation.

Rambhau enjoyed listening, but when David asked him to trust Christ as his Savior, the pearl diver always shook his head, replying, "Your Christian way to heaven is too easy; I can't accept it. If I gained entrance to heaven in that way, I'd feel like a beggar who'd been admitted out of pity. I want to earn my place in heaven, so I'm going to *work* for it."

As the years went by, nothing the missionary

---

*A guide on pages 91-93 is provided to help in pronunciation of unfamiliar words.

said could change Rambhau's thinking. One evening the missionary heard a knock on his door. It was Rambhau.

"Come in, dear friend," the missionary invited.

"No, Sahib," said the pearl diver. "You must come to my house. I have something to show you. Please don't refuse."

"Of course, I'll come."

As the two men neared Rambhau's cabin, the pearl diver said, "In a week I'll start working for my place in heaven. I'm leaving for Delhi, and I'm going there on my knees."

"Man, you're crazy! It's 900 miles to Delhi! The skin on your knees will tear, and you will get blood poisoning or leprosy before you get halfway."

"No, I must crawl to Delhi," Rambhau insisted. "The immortals will reward me, and the suffering will be sweet—purchasing heaven for me!"

"My friend, you can't do this. How can I let you do it when Jesus Christ has suffered and died to purchase heaven for you?"

But the old man would not be dissuaded. "You're my dearest friend, Sahib. Through the years you have stood by me in sickness and in need. At times, you were my only friend. But even you can't change me from my plan to purchase eternal bliss. I *must* go to Delhi."

Inside the hut, Morse was seated in the chair Rambhau had built for him, where on many occasions he'd read the Bible. Rambhau left the room and returned with a small but heavy strongbox. "I've had this box for years," he said. "I keep only one thing in it. Now I'll tell you about it, Sahib. Once I had a son . . ."

"A son! Rambhau, you never before said a word about a son!"

"No, Sahib, I couldn't." The diver's eyes became moist. "Now, I must tell you, because soon I'll leave, and who knows whether I'll ever come back. My son was a diver—the best pearl diver on the coasts of India. He had the swiftest dive, the keenest eyes, the strongest arms, and the longest breath of any diver who ever sought for pearls. What joy he brought me!

"Most pearls have some blemish that only an expert can detect. But my son dreamed of finding the perfect pearl—beyond any that had ever been found. One day he found it. But he'd been under water too long. That pearl cost him his life, and he died soon afterward."

**The gem blazed in brilliance
beyond all cultured pearls.**

The old diver bowed his head, his body shaking, but there was no sound. "All these years," he continued, "I have kept this pearl. But now I'm going and may not return, and to you, my friend, I'm giving my pearl."

The old man opened the strongbox and took out a carefully wrapped bundle. Gently opening the package, he brought forth an immense pearl and placed it in the missionary's hand. The gem blazed in brilliance beyond all cultured pearls. It would bring a fabulous price on any market.

For a moment the missionary was speechless, gazing in awe. "Rambhau! What a pearl!" he exclaimed.

"That pearl, Sahib, is *perfect*," the old man quietly replied.

"This is a wonderful, amazing pearl. Let me buy it. I'll give you $10,000 for it."

"Sahib! Are you crazy?"

"OK, I'll give you $15,000 for it, or if it takes more—I will *work* for it."

"This pearl is beyond price. No one in the world has enough money to pay what this gem is worth to me. A million dollars would not buy it. I won't sell it to you, but I'll *give* it to you."

"No, Rambhau, I cannot accept it. As much as I want the pearl, I cannot accept it that way. Perhaps I'm too proud, but that's too easy. I must *pay* for it, or *work* for it . . ."

The old man was stunned. "You don't understand. Don't you see? My only son gave his life to get this pearl, and I won't sell it for any amount of money. Its value is in the lifeblood of my son. I cannot sell it, but I'll *give* it to you. Accept it as a token of my love for you."

David Morse could not speak for a moment. Then he gripped the old man's hand.

"Rambhau," he said in a low voice, "don't you see? My words are just what you have been saying to God."

The diver looked long and searchingly at the missionary. Then . . . slowly . . . he began to understand.

"God is offering you salvation as a free *gift*," said the missionary. "It's so great, so priceless, no man on earth can buy it. Millions of dollars are too little—an insult to God the Father.

"No man on earth can *earn* salvation. No man is good enough to *deserve* it. It cost God the lifeblood of His only Son to gain for you an entrance into heaven. In a million years, in a hundred pilgrimages, you cannot *earn* that entrance. All you can do is to *accept* it as a token of God's love for you—a sinner.

Some things are too priceless to be bought or earned. I will accept His gift!

"Of course, I'll accept the pearl in deep humility, praying to God that I may be worthy of your love. Rambhau, won't you accept God's great gift of heaven, in deep humility, knowing it cost Him the death of His Son?"

Tears began rolling down the cheeks of the old diver.

"Sahib, I see it now. I've believed in the truth of Jesus for the last two years, but I couldn't believe that His salvation was free. Now I understand. Some things are too priceless to be bought or earned. I will accept His gift!"

In the Christian's task of evangelizing all the people of the world for whom Christ died, many faithful witnesses like David Morse are needed. People need to know that Christians care enough to invest time and effort in them as David did with Rambhau. Our world of more than 6 billion people must be brought to Christ—usually one person at a time.

In the work of the eternal harvest, many hands are needed to do various kinds of labor: preparing the soil . . . planting the seed . . . watering the fields . . . toiling with patience and grace. These hands must labor with intensity and urgency, yet knowing that God alone gives the harvest.

The following pages briefly tell several stories of hands in harvest fields of the Far East. They are Filipino, Japanese, Korean, ethnic Lisu from Tibet, and one anonymous nationality. Their backgrounds and salvation experiences differ, but their love for the Lord and commitment to the work of His harvest are great. Their lives prove the principle that the missionary Paul proclaims, "Remember this: Whoever sows sparingly will also reap sparingly, and whoever sows generously will also reap generously" (2 Corinthians 9:6).

1

Luz—Sowing in Tears but Reaping with Joy

Those who plant in tears will harvest with shouts of joy. They weep as they go to plant their seed, but they sing as they return with the harvest (Psalm 126:5-6, NLT).

"Dead? Vern is dead?" Luz spoke with disbelief. "It . . . it can't be . . . true! And . . . and what about . . . my . . . my sons? And . . . and the others?" The Filipino lady struggled for words, her outward demeanor failing to reflect her inner emotions.

Luz Tamayo had just learned her husband had died instantly in a highway tragedy. Two of their sons, Virgil and Sam, along with two other young men from their church, had been in the vehicle, but they had survived. The date was February 6, 1999.

Rev. Vern Tamayo was the district superintendent of the Metro Manila District in the Philippines, appointed by General Superintendent Donald Owens just three years before. At the time Vern accepted this challenge, he turned Miracle Church of the Nazarene over to a younger pastor. He then took on Taytay First Church, which had declined greatly. Its size did not present a work overload, however, since only 10 people in addition to his family showed up the first Sunday.

Luz and their three sons labored with tireless enthusiasm to support Vern's efforts to bring revival to the district. He met with the pastors every Monday to encourage them, teach them leadership and church growth principles, and lead them in intercession for the harvest. He challenged every church that was not yet self-supporting to take a leap of faith to become self-supporting. The churches rose to the challenge, propelling the district to regular district status.

The district grew rapidly. Many workers who had completed their studies and served the required ministry internship were ordained at the next district assembly. Yet, in the midst of the district's financial and numerical growth, the Tamayos experienced a setback. During a Philippine economic crisis, their bank failed, bringing their family enormous financial loss.

But that misfortune did not deter this man of God. In his last year, Vern spoke often about the vision God gave him of a Metro Manila Nazarene church with more than 1,000 members. Through his sons' growing-up years, he etched on their imaginations gripping images of a vast urgent harvest to reap, with the prospect of reaping outside the existing Nazarene field.

But now, Vern was gone. This gifted pastor and leader, this beloved husband and father, was dead—

his life snuffed out quickly and unexpectedly by a fatal accident. The sudden death of a minister who blazed with evangelistic passion sent shock waves throughout the Nazarene world.

═══════════

Lucinda (Luz) Fernandez grew up in Manila, capital of the Philippines, in a devout Christian home. Her mom faithfully read Bible stories to her. At six years of age Luz put her trust in Jesus as her personal Savior, although the church her family attended did not put it in those terms.

Luz grew in grace, her joy knowing no bounds. She drew close to Christ, often dreaming about the Lord she loved and a life of service for Him. When she was 12, her 57-year-old father answered God's call to pastoral ministry. Luz's love for Christ deepened as she became involved in the life of the church.

While studying for a bachelor of science degree at Manila's Mapua Institute of Technology, Luz made a complete commitment to Christ during a revival campaign. An evangelism and discipleship team came to Knox Methodist Church that hosted three events for all the congregations of the area.

The series began with a 10-day revival in which many people came to faith in Christ and assurance of their salvation. At the close of the revival, a celebration included testimonies by everyone who had prayed through. "I will follow the Lord always," Luz boldly declared.

The evangelism and discipleship team held an

intensive follow-up seminar for everyone who had taken steps of faith. It was titled "Wanted: Ten Brave Christians." In that seminar, Luz accepted God's call to be a courageous Christian witness.

The final team event was discipleship training. During the weekly sessions, Luz's roots went deep into Christ and into God's Word. Her folks retired from pastoral ministry, moved to Antipolo, and became involved in the Antipolo Methodist Church.

In her love for boys and girls, Luz became an effective soul winner and discipler.

Zealous for her Lord and surprised there was no Sunday School for children, Luz went to the pastor to ask permission to start a class. He welcomed her help. In fact, Benjamin Manuel had graduated from Luzon Nazarene Bible College (LNBC), having been converted under Nazarene missionary John Pattee. In doctrine and spirit, Benjamin was one with Nazarenes.

Luz looked far and wide for children. Seeing them playing under mango trees or shooting basketball hoops, she talked with them and convinced them to join her. Soon she had 40 kids coming to Sunday School. In her love for boys and girls, Luz became an effective soul winner and discipler.

At church, Luz saw Vern Tamayo, who was in rebellion against God. His parents were lay missionaries, sent by the Taytay Methodist Church to help strengthen its sister congregation in Antipolo. Vern drove them to church but stayed in the car, reading the newspaper during services.

Luz started a Methodist Youth Fellowship (MYF) for young people in their early 20s. The pastor was so delighted when she got Vern involved that he sent Vern and the entire group to the Nazarene youth camp on the LNBC campus. There, Vern came to Christ and caught fire for the Lord. He began bringing friends to MYF meetings in Antipolo, and within a year the group soared to about 100 young adults. The vibrant group of growing Christians elected him MYF president.

An attraction between Vern and Luz grew as they served the Lord together. After a year and a half of organizing and leading events and evangelistic outreach, he proposed marriage to her. He later admitted that part of his pushing for so many church activities was so he would have more opportunities to be with his special friend.

Vern and Luz married in November 1975. A year later the Tamayos welcomed a son, Virgil. The baby brought great joy, helping counteract the sorrow they felt when the Methodist district superintendent removed Pastor Manuel from Antipolo Church and replaced him with a theologically liberal pastor. Before long, the Tamayos switched to the Taytay Methodist Church.

In 1978 their second son, Ezekiel, was born, and hope for a suitable church home was born in their heart. Their former pastor introduced the Tamayos

Luz and Vern Tamayo at Luzon Nazarene Bible College, 1995

to Peter Burkhart, Nazarene missionary, who told them a Nazarene church would be planted in Taytay. Peter asked them to seek God's will about helping to establish a strong holiness church. God led them to say yes, and they began working with the missionary and Norie Mateo, a Filipino church leader, in a series of evangelistic crusades.

Vern found several locations, made all arrangements, and even played the accordion. The crusades gave birth to Taytay First Church of the Nazarene, which began worship services in Community Savings and Loan Bank, a financial institution Vern's grandfather founded and Vern now led. In August 1979 Luz and Vern became charter members. Six months later, they welcomed to their home a third son, Samuel.

Eduardo Laurea became pastor, and in the latter part of 1979, the Tamayos helped him with evangelistic outreach to Antipolo to plant a church near where Luz's parents were living. In December of that year, with the group meeting in Sumulong High School, the district superintendent organized Antipolo Church of the Nazarene.

Each Sunday, Pastor Laurea and the Tamayos led worship in the mornings at Taytay First Church and in the afternoons at the Antipolo church. During the week, Luz and Vern led Bible studies in homes and on vacant lots in both towns. Soon Antipolo got its own pastor.

In 1982, the Antipolo Church acquired property, and Work and Witness teams from the Sacramento District in the United States came to help with construction of a sanctuary. When the pastor announced he was returning to Bible college, Luz and Vern accepted interim leadership for the church.

Later that year missionary Kyle Green, director of campus development at Asia-Pacific Nazarene Theological Seminary (APNTS), added preaching responsibilities at Antipolo to his ministries. Since Kyle's previous service in the Philippines was in another language area, Vern served as his interpreter. Rev. Green's tenure at Antipolo was brief, as he soon concluded his missionary career.

When Gordon Gibson replaced Kyle at APNTS in 1984, the Antipolo church asked him to be their pastor. Gordon and Vern became close brothers in

Christ and partners in ministry. In 1987, however, when Metro Manila District leaders decided only Filipinos would serve as senior pastors, Gordon and Vern's roles reversed; Vern became senior pastor and Gordon the assistant.

In 1985, with Rev. Gibson's gentle but persistent persuasion, Luz and Vern enrolled at APNTS. Financially they could attend, since they were part owners of a small bank. Due to their church-plant-

Rev. Vern Tamayo preaching at Miracle Church of the Nazarene

ing efforts between 1983 and 1995, however, they did not complete their master's degree programs. (Luz lacks only a thesis to receive her master of religious education degree.)

Under the Tamayos' leadership, the Antipolo congregation established church-planting teams. Luz and Vern were catalysts in transplanting human "seedlings" from Antipolo to the Laguna area where the Bugarin, Pidilla, Tanay, Morong, Teresa, and Baras churches took root. Plus, on the edges of Antipolo, they helped teams to slip human Nazarene "seedlings" into soil that produced the Cogeo Calvary, Bethany, and Grace churches. A young man they sponsored through Visayan Nazarene Bible College (VNBC) later helped complete the planting of the Valenzuela Church of the Nazarene in Manila.

In 1988, Luz and Vern began to sponsor Bible college students' education to prepare for the work of the harvest, paying for eight Filipinos to attend LNBC and three to attend APNTS that year. In the next decade they paid for 10 students a year to go to VNBC.

In 1991, they handed over Antipolo Nazarene Church to a full-time pastor, Vern having been bivocational and only able to devote part time to pastoral duties. They began to concentrate on strengthening the many churches they had helped to plant.

In late 1995 Luz and Vern turned their attention to Taytay. While striving to save their bank during a national financial crisis, they surveyed the prospects for planting more Nazarene churches in Vern's hometown. The next year, they led a nucleus of Nazarenes in planting Miracle Church in Taytay's Muzon section. In less than a year, Miracle Church planted the Bangiad Church in the Thessalonians subdivision of Taytay.

The "seedling" had quickly produced a harvest.

The Tamayos continued crusade strategies they had used for a dozen years. Their sons—Virgil, Kel (Ezekiel), and Sam—were musicians in the crusades. Vern formed and led a band, playing the guitar and training other instrumentalists, as well as instilling confidence in the lead singer and backup group.

Seed sowing, watering, and weeding out hindrances to the harvest developed Miracle Church and Bangiad Church into strong congregations. Despite Miracle Church's first building resembling a barn, its average worship attendance soared to 200. The "seedling" had quickly produced a harvest. Sowing, watering, and weeding continued, and there was a 100-fold harvest.

Vern's death left the district without its leader, Taytay First Church without a pastor, three sons without a dad, and Luz without a spouse and best friend. Though their lives were reduced to ashes, Luz knew that God would help her and her "boys." The prophet Isaiah had announced that God comforts those who mourn and bestows on them "beauty instead of ashes" (Isaiah 61:3). The grieving Tamayo family found this to be true for them.

Rather than dropping out of God's service, too devastated to go on, Luz clung to her Lord and His unfailing love. He had never forsaken her and would not forsake her now.

The church board asked Luz to become the pastor. The newly elected district superintendent and the field director urged her to accept the invitation. She took the matter before the Lord, and the answer came that she should accept the call, confident that the Holy Spirit would help her.

"One of the reasons I accepted the invitation was to help my children to see the fulfillment of Vern's vision of a great church," Luz testifies. "I believe that in my lifetime I will see Vern's dream become a reality." Having completed all ordination re-

Luz Tamayo (standing second from right) at ordination

quirements and after being approved by the District Ministerial Credentials Board, General Superintendent Paul Cunningham ordained Luz in March 2000 amid tearful rejoicing.

Taytay First Church's building has filled with people and overflowed both its upstairs and downstairs areas. An English-speaking Nazarene congregation had used the same facilities at a different time on Sundays, but that congregation moved to a new location, giving First Church exclusive use of its facilities.

Under Luz's leadership Taytay First Church has four Sunday worship services and church school both on Sunday and on Saturday. With over 600 people, the church is well on its way to realizing Vern's dream of a church with 1,000 or more people. A recent Vacation Bible School had 123 "graduates," and another VBS followed for many more children.

Since Luz is related to many motocross racers, God gave the Tamayos compassion for the racers.

Luz's heart burns with soul-winning passion as she, her sons, and her people sow salvation seeds through high school outreach, concert and motocross evangelism, catalytic church planting, and more. In partnership with Nazarene Health Care Fellowship, Luz leads First Church in one-day medical missions to reach people for Christ. More than 100 people have come to the Savior in a single day in response to personal evangelism by those she has trained.

———

Long before Vern's death, the Taytay hometown hero was Ernie Leongson, East Asia's motocross champion. The Tamayos took their sons to races and exhibitions that drew Filipino movie stars and other celebrities. Since Luz is related to many motocross racers, God gave the Tamayos compassion for the racers, especially those who were injured in smashups.

The Tamayo boys began racing. Virgil became the Philippine National Amateur Motocross Champion, and Vern became chaplain for the team. On race days Christians wore logos, displayed bike decals to declare God's glory, and prayed together before each race. They broadcast Christian music, quoted scripture over the PA system, and gave their testimonies. They earned the respect of other team members and led many of them to Christ.

Virgil, Kel, and Sam had taken music lessons, and that training began to pay off. They discovered that many people won through motocross evangelism had music ability. So they formed the Nazarene Praise Band that receives many invitations to play, sing, and give their testimonies.

Mel Aquino, a popular racing star, came to Christ and into Taytay First Church. He soon led his mother and all six of his brothers and sisters to the Savior and into the church and its ministries. Mel is the lead singer for the Praise Band.

Today, Taytay Church overflows with young

people who travel to minister musically, proclaim the way of salvation, and win hundreds to Christ. They lead "Religion Day" at high schools, making it a fun event for students. They invite youth to accept Christ, and often everyone comes to pray. The next day, many are in church. On the Sunday after Vern was killed, 50 youth who had been in membership classes were received into Taytay First Church's membership.

Virgil, a college graduate, is serving the Lord

Luz Tamayo with sons: Virgil in front, Sam on left, Kel on right

along with his mom and brothers. Kel has graduated from a civil engineering college, and Sam will graduate soon. Sam has answered God's call to preach, taking up the mantle of his father in holiness evangelism, and he plans to attend APNTS.

Luz and Vern shared over 25 years of seed sowing, faithful watering, and reaping the harvest. None who knew them ever imagined that Vern would have left Luz so soon—leaving the urgent harvest with one less worker. Satan intended it for evil, but the God who is far greater is giving beauty instead of ashes.

Luz Tamayo, her sons, and her people keep going forth to sow seeds of full salvation, watering them with their tears. Claiming promises recorded in Psalm 126:5-6, they keep coming back from the fields with shouts of joy, carrying bundles of harvested grain—thousands of Filipinos who will become more hands for the ripening harvest.

2

Hitoshi— Planting and Reaping in the Land of the Rising Sun

You will always reap what you sow! . . . But those who live to please the Spirit will harvest everlasting life from the Spirit. So don't get tired of doing what is good. Don't get discouraged and give up, for we will reap a harvest of blessing at the appropriate time (Galatians 6:7-9, NLT).

Hitoshi awakened, disturbed by his dream. He saw himself in minister's attire in front of a church with children gathered around him. Puzzled by the dream's meaning, the Buddhist teen decided to visit the nearby Catholic church that looked like the church in his nighttime "vision."

"How can I become a minister like you?" the high school senior asked the priest.

"You must attend Sophia University," the minister responded, referring to the famous Jesuit school in Tokyo.

Hitoshi Fukue entered the university to study English literature. Though religion classes were offered, he was not exposed to the gospel. There were many international students with whom he could converse; therefore, his ability in English soared. He met foreigners who came to teach or study for the summer, including Helen Wilson and Thelma Culver, dean of women and academic dean respectively of Northwest Nazarene College (now University).

"Would you like to study in the United States?" Miss Wilson asked Hitoshi.

"Certainly, but I can't leave here now," he replied. Taking her business card, he went to his room, stuck it in a drawer, and put it out of his mind.

The time was the late '60s when a Japan-wide student revolt was under way. Protests and conflicts pervaded university campuses. In his junior year, Hitoshi tired of the turmoil. Feeling no hope for the future, he recalled the card that Helen Wilson had given to him two years earlier. He found it tucked in a back corner of his desk.

―――――

Hitoshi had never heard such strange and shocking words.

―――――

Addressing an envelope, Hitoshi thought, *I wonder if she'll remember me?* Although he wrote to tell

Miss Wilson about his desire to study at Northwest Nazarene College (NNC), he doubted that she would respond.

To his surprise, a reply came quickly, expressing genuine concern for him. Helen ended her letter by inviting him to come with the promise, "I will consider you to be my son." Hitoshi had never heard such strange and shocking words.

Why would this Japanese young man find such a statement "strange and shocking"?

———

Hitoshi was born on small Shikoku Island, south of Japan's main islands. In his elementary school days, his mother left their family because of marital problems. Hitoshi, his nine-year-old sister, and three-year-old brother remained with their father, a short-fused man who often unleashed his anger against them.

Hitoshi's mother found work in another area of the island and came to visit her children only once every two weeks. She came to their rooms late at night to talk with them, but she was never there when they got up the next morning. The children grew up without sharing meals with their mom and without seeing their parents talking with one another.

The Fukue home had many Buddhist statues and symbols. Their father had set aside one small room for objects of worship. And even though he paid priests to come to conduct memorial services to honor ancestors, it made no difference in his daily life.

When Hitoshi was in the sixth grade, his sister asked him and their little brother if they wanted to move in with their mother, and they agreed. Their mother had succeeded in business, and now she could afford to take care of them. She set a date for them to go to school as on any other day, being careful not to do anything to disclose their plan. They left as usual that morning, rushing to the train station in a soaking rain. It was the beginning of Typhoon Isewan, one of the deadliest storms in Japan's history. Mrs. Fukue was waiting for them in a taxi.

The children were happy at last to be with their mother, yet frightened that their dad would come and take them back. Mrs. Fukue had rented a hideaway apartment, and the kids entered new schools. But in only two weeks, their dad located them. He met with each child in the school office to ask if he or she wanted to stay with their mother or to come home with him.

Hitoshi was so emotional he couldn't answer; he could only cry. For the first time, he saw his father weep. His dad left without him and never came to visit the family again. The boy felt his father had abandoned him—completely.

The kind offer from a near stranger in America touched Hitoshi. Few students, in those days, left Japan to study in the United States. He kept wondering why Miss Wilson would offer to sponsor him legally, help him financially, and assist him in other ways. And, above all, treat him as her son.

Hitoshi accepted Helen Wilson's offer with gratitude and excitement. Upon arriving in Nampa, Idaho, he found that she, Thelma Culver, and other NNC people were eager to be his family. Helen arranged an international student scholarship plus a grant from a Rotary Club, which together covered one-third of his school bill. His family in Japan matched that amount, and he got a job at the college cafeteria to cover his room and board.

Everyone called him Paul—and Paul he became. He experienced the goodwill and ready acceptance of administrators, teachers, and students. Miss Wilson counseled him as though she were his mother. Such kindness produced a hunger in him to know more about the Christian faith.

Dr. Hitoshi Paul Fukue

Paul attended worship services at College Church where Jim Bond [now General Superintendent Bond] was senior pastor. Going twice on Sundays, on Wednesday evenings, and to college chapel services, he tried to grasp what it was all about, but he became discouraged. Something seemed to hinder him.

I don't know if there is a God, he thought, besieged by doubts. *If there is, I must find and follow Him. If there is no God, then I'll give up on it all.*

One November Sunday evening in 1968, Paul's struggle intensified. He resolved to find God that night or to give up trying. At the close of his message, the missionary speaker opened the altar, inviting people to commit their lives to God for service. Paul didn't understand what all this meant; yet, not knowing how he got there, he found himself kneeling at the altar.

"It was like an out-of-body experience," Paul testifies.

A sharp sense of his own sinfulness stabbed him. In the midst of unspeakable light, Hitoshi Paul Fukue saw such evil in his own heart that he felt he deserved death. Yet he sensed mercy, forgiveness, and grace flowing to him. He would never forget the dual revelations of his sinfulness and God's mercy.

"It was like an out-of-body experience," Paul testifies. "When I came to myself, I was reassured as joy inundated my heart. When I went outside, I looked at the stars, the trees, and the whole world around me. Everything was beautiful!"

Paul walked to his dorm room without telling anyone what had happened to him. But he couldn't stop thinking about the promise he'd made to himself: *I won't ever go back.* He was terrified, yet comforted by God's powerful, loving presence.

This transforming experience helped him know he was now a new creation in Christ. He began to search the Scriptures and to devour devotional books. Bart McKay and Phyllis Hartley [now Perkins], who formerly had served in Japan, gave Paul a Japanese Bible and gospel literature. He grew by leaps and bounds in his newfound faith and intimate walk with the Savior.

Rev. Bond's preaching laid a firm foundation on which Paul built his Christian belief system. After participating in classes to prepare believers for baptism and membership, Paul was baptized, and he joined the church. A wonderful mentoring relationship developed between Pastor Bond and Paul.

As Christmas break approached, Paul wondered, *What will I do when the other students leave for the holidays? I sure can't go home.*

"Would you like to join our Work and Witness team?" a fellow student asked him. "About 20 of us are going to Arizona for a week to complete a sanctuary for a congregation."

Paul signed up. Traveling in trucks and vans loaded with materials and tools, it took three days to get to Douglas, a Mexican-American community in southern Arizona. Overjoyed in giving himself to serve others, Paul sensed God calling him to Christian service. At a dedication service for the new building, he prayed, "Lord, I want the kind of future that will give me joy like this. Make my life eternally significant for You."

In the following days Paul kept seeking God's will for his immediate and long-range future. Beneath a tree one night, he prayed fervently: "Lead my life, Lord. I'm all yours. Use me as you choose." A marvelous sense of peace flooded him as he resolved to change his major and prepare for ministry. He threw himself with abandon into his studies under such godly guides as Morris Weigelt and A. E. Sanner.

In his junior year, Paul's sweetheart, Mitsuko, left Japan to study in Canada, stopping briefly at Nampa to visit him. Unhappy in her college, Mitsuko and Paul prayed about a way for her also to study at NNC.

A Nazarene physician in Nampa offered to sponsor Mitsuko with the needed documents and guarantees. Arriving in Idaho, she lived in the home of the Grady Cantrells. Previously, she had been baptized and started her walk with the Lord in Japan. Now, with the help of Christians in the Nampa Nazarene community, her faith grew firm.

Paul and Mitsuko forged wonderful friendships at NNC and with College Church members. They were married at the church right after Paul's graduation. The Grady Cantrells, Helen Wilson, Thelma Culver, and many others labored to make it a lovely wedding.

The newlyweds went to Kansas City for Paul to study at Nazarene Theological Seminary and Mitsuko at MidAmerica Nazarene College (now University). She would be in the first graduating class in 1972. Early in their three years in the Kansas City area, they started a Japanese Christian fellowship at Nall Avenue Church of the Nazarene. The Fukues served a joyous Japanese people, most of whom were married to American spouses. Following the conversion of 70-year-old Mrs. Suzuki under their ministry, they celebrated God's transforming grace as Gary Moore sang "How Great Thou Art" in Japanese, and Mrs. Suzuki received believer baptism.

When both Paul and Mitsuko graduated, they prayed to know God's will for them next. They sensed His leading them to return to Japan. Arriving in Tokyo in the summer of 1973, they contacted Nazarene leaders of the Japan District. Superintendent Harada was kind to them as a Japanese couple who became Nazarenes abroad and then returned to serve in Japan. In some cases where this had happened, Japanese churches had not seemed anxious to welcome such "outsiders."

They stayed temporarily with Paul's mom in Kochi City, hoping that Paul would be called to be an associate pastor, but it did not happen. After they had been there a short time, Paul became ill, quickly going from bad to worse. When paralysis set in, he was rushed by ambulance to the hospital. The cause of the illness remains a mystery even to this day.

During Paul's recovery, he read a book that God used to inspire him to pray about pioneering a church. Searching the Bible for a clear word, he came to Haggai 1:8, which says: "Go up into the mountains and bring down timber and build the house, so that I may take pleasure in it and be honored."

When Paul's strength returned, he and Mitsuko looked for a place for planting the Church of the Nazarene. In November 1973, they bought a small house with help from their parents. It became their home and worship center, as well as a place to earn their livelihood—teaching English to neighborhood children. Their home was a true multipurpose facility.

Through seven years of planting the church, people came and the church grew. The need for a sanctuary grew, and so did the Fukue family. Their son, Tomoki, arrived in 1975. Four years later their daughter, Airi, increased the Fukue family's size and joy.

God used the Fukues to lead Paul's sister to Christ, then his mother, brother, and brother-in-law.

Paul and Mitsuko Fukue with Airi, daughter, and Tomoki, son

Later his father-in-law came to Christ, as well as Mitsuko's brother and mother. Many others came to the Lord through their ministry.

In 1979 the land's value was about 50 million yen (U.S. $200,000).

Both the congregation and the pastoral family felt the need for a separate church facility. But first they needed land, which was extremely expensive. Paul's brother-in-law, now his brother in Christ also, had a compelling dream one night in which he saw a church building on land that he owned. It was a heavenly vision for him. The next morning, he told his wife they would give their property for the Church of the Nazarene. In 1979 the land's value was about 50 million yen (U.S. $200,000). A miracle!

In the early years of planting the Church of the Nazarene in Kochi City, Hitoshi's mother, who had studied under a famous Japanese ventriloquist, started a Christian ventriloquism ministry. She continued for many years, serving in churches, schools, hospitals, and homes.

After the church building was completed and the congregation was strong and growing, Hitoshi sensed the Lord leading him to pursue further studies. He and Mitsuko sought God's will, and he announced their plans to the district superintendent, who found an interim pastor for the church. Then the Fukue family left for Boston University in America where Paul worked on a doctorate of theology and Mitsuko earned a master's degree in education.

Their three years in the Boston area went quickly for them. As clearly as the Lord had led them to graduate studies, He led them to return to their church. The congregation rejoiced to have them back. Paul worked on his doctoral dissertation as he led the church in outreach. After his dissertation was completed and accepted, Boston University conferred upon him the Th.D. degree.

Altogether, including their time in Boston, the Fukues' ministry in Kochi extended across 20 years, from 1973 until 1993. They expected to stay for many more years. So it came as a surprise in the fall

Nazarene leaders in Japan. Paul Fukue, standing far left. Regional Director Brent Cobb, seated in middle.

of 1992 when Paul received a call about taking a different pastorate. The district superintendent, pastor of the Oyamadai Church, wanted Paul to replace him when he soon retired.

As Paul searched the Scriptures, God clearly spoke to him from the words of the prophet Nathan to David: "Whatever you have in mind, do it, for God is with you" (1 Chronicles 17:2). After much prayer, Paul knew the move was God's will.

In early 1993, the Fukues left the more rural setting of Kochi for Tokyo, a city of 13 million people. "Our lives were deeply rooted in the soil of Kochi," Paul says. "We had close relationships with the people there." Oyamadai Church is the Mrs. Florence Eckel Memorial Church, which honors a pioneer Nazarene missionary in Japan.

The Fukues fell in love with the people of that great, historic congregation, and the people quickly took them to their hearts. Deep, strong relationships between the church family and the pastoral family developed. Paul, Mitsuko, and their children enjoyed a rich ministry and found much fulfillment at Oyamadai, a church of considerable influence.

The choir director, Makoto Ibuka, is the son of the former head of Sony Corporation. Dick Sano, president of Buena Vista Videos, a branch of the Walt Disney Corporation of Japan, is president of Oyamadai Church's men's fellowship and chairman of the evangelism committee. Mr. Hirota, a godly layman, is an executive for Dunkin' Donuts and the Yoshinoya Restaurant chain.

For years, Dr. Fukue was an adjunct faculty

member of Asia-Pacific Nazarene Theological Seminary (APNTS), going to Manila every May to teach. Additionally, he taught at Japan Nazarene Theological Seminary in Tokyo and served during a crisis time as president of Japan Christian Junior College (JCJC), a Nazarene educational institution. Today he serves full time as a key professor at APNTS. Mitsuko also teaches at the same school.

The Lord has brought great things to pass through Hitoshi Paul Fukue. Three generations of Japanese are serving Jesus today because of what God's grace has accomplished through the life of this godly man. Many more lives continue to be changed because he and Mitsuko are channels through which Christ's Spirit is flowing life-giving water to make seeds grow for a harvest for God's glory.

3

Stephen*— Laboring in a Hard Field Among Fierce Foes

I am sending you out like sheep among wolves. Therefore be shrewd as snakes and as innocent as doves (Matthew 10:16).

"We'll break in if your pastor doesn't come out!" the villagers yelled, pounding on the walls of the house and demanding the blood of the Christians.

More than 100 screaming people surrounded Stephen's house during worship. Brandishing sickles, knives, spears, and torches, they shouted and waved letters from city leaders ordering the church to close and never reopen. The little flock was terrified; yet, when the crowd called their shepherd out, some of them wanted to go in his place.

---

*Stephen's name and the people among whom he works have been changed for security reasons.

When Pastor Stephen went out to plead for the safety of his congregation, the angry crowd told him it was their last church service.

"But I have the legal documents that grant us permission to hold worship services," Stephen said. "It's from the head of the Christian division of the Department of Religion for the province."

"We don't care if you have permission from the president," the persecutors shot back. "If you hold one more service, we'll destroy your home."

====

An angry, rock-wielding mob filled the yard.

====

The mob demanded that Stephen finish the final worship service in one hour. When Stephen reported this to his people inside, they decided to pray for an hour and then to begin meeting secretly in the homes of believers.

The next day, when Stephen stepped out of his house, people were waiting to follow him. If he went to one of his member's homes, it would endanger the family. When his wife went to buy food, they followed her. Eventually they did visit a believer's home, and an angry, rock-wielding mob filled the yard.

====

Years earlier, Stephen's parents had opened their home as a place of worship. A graduate of a Nazarene Bible college labored with the couple to plant a church in their village. All the family members soon trusted Jesus as their Savior—except Stephen. He was the lone holdout.

During worship times he hid in his bedroom but listened as the fast-growing congregation sang with gusto and prayed for him by name. Finally, Stephen could stand it no longer; he committed his heart and life to Christ.

Stephen became the pastor's right-hand man, going with him to preaching outposts, carrying the lantern and songbooks. Gifted musically, Stephen sang special songs and played the guitar.

One day, while reading the apostle Paul's testimony, Stephen was moved by the missionary's confession and felt compelled to preach the gospel. The words seemed to leap from the page as God used them to call him into full-time ministry.

Nazarene congregation in Stephen's country

Stephen went to a Nazarene theological school. There, God spoke to him about taking seeds of salvation to a major, yet-to-be-evangelized ethnic group.

Upon graduation, Stephen and his family went forth with a burning desire to plant the Church of the Nazarene among the Mundanese, one of the world's largest unreached people groups. Many college and district leaders, as well as his fellow graduates, doubted that he would succeed. Though the Mundanese are generally gracious, the "soil" of most of their hearts is extremely resistant to seeds of the gospel.

Steeped in superstition, these people have often persecuted and sometimes killed Christians who tried to convert them. When an occasional Mundanese person has come to the Lamb of God, he or she has generally become like a lamb among wolves. The new convert's family has cast out the "traitor."

So strong was Stephen's sense of *call* to the Mundanese that he refused to see *impossibilities*. He saw the people, rather, as God does—people needing the Savior to give them a future and hope. He and his family went to live among them and offer them the joy that is in Jesus.

Bible college teachers and district leaders wondered if they would ever hear from this family again. For a long time it was as though they had disappeared. But God always knew where they were. And they had a prayer partner in the Bible college principal's wife, a fourth-generation Christian Mundanese.

Stephen's sense of urgency was compelling.

God spoke to him, even from rather obscure scripture. Words jumped from the pages of his Bible: "If you wait until the wind and weather are just right, you will never plant anything and never harvest anything" (Ecclesiastes 11:4, TEV).

He moved his family into a Mundanese city and began to show Christ's love to the people. There were disappointments and discouraging events, but

Seekers of Christ in the country where Stephen serves

Stephen soon led a Mundanese man to Christ, setting off a celestial celebration by heaven's angels!

God gave more converts, and Stephen had a few sheep to shepherd. The little flock enjoyed placid pasturage for a while, but when they applied for a building permit, their application was rejected. So Stephen and his family kept leading worship in their tiny rented house. Newborn Christians were jeered and threatened, but they faithfully came to pray, praise, and prepare to serve the Lord.

One Sunday thugs surrounded the house where they normally met, but the little congregation was not there. Stephen had told the members to meet at the beach for a day of worship and family celebration. While they were worshiping under coconut trees, a mob surrounded the house church, enraged that no one was there as usual. When Stephen got home, they came to threaten him and gave the ultimatum: "Stop holding services or we'll destroy your home."

Persecution took a toll on the pastor's family and flock. They were in serious danger. Stephen started having health problems, including a stroke that left much of his left side paralyzed. The harassment and her husband's broken health burdened Stephen's wife, and she pleaded to move back to their hometown. Once there, they prayed and sought God's will.

But their hearts yearned for the baby Christians they'd left behind. They sent a new Bible school graduate to be interim pastor to the small congregation. Since he was unknown in that city, he was not followed when he visited the people. He found them to be true disciples. They were discouraged but not defeated as they rotated their worship from house to house.

With a radiant face, he came to district assembly, having miraculously regained use of his left side.

In the following four months, Stephen's family interceded for those they had left, writing to them often, encouraging them with such Pauline prayers as: "I pray that out of his glorious riches he may strengthen you with power through his Spirit in your inner being, so that Christ may dwell in your hearts through faith. And I pray that you, being rooted and established in love, may have power, together with all the saints, to grasp how wide and long and high and deep is the love of Christ" (Ephesians 3:16-18).

God restored Stephen's health. With a radiant face, he went to the district assembly, having miraculously regained use of his left side. His family was ready to go back to the Mundanese, unafraid of facing struggles and hardships.

Soon after returning to the Mundanese, Stephen and his wife were riding a motorcycle in ministry work when a truck struck them from behind. Seriously injured, Stephen's helpmate lay unconscious in the hospital for six days. Even though the law required that the driver pay for their motorcycle repair and medical expenses, the truck operator refused.

Stephen's policeman brother came from his town to help recover the motorcycle the local police had impounded. While dealing with them, the brother insisted that the driver pay for repairs and medical costs for treatment of his sister-in-law. But a local policeman warned him, "The man who hit your brother knows him well; in fact, he's one of his neighbors. If you demand compensation, we will attack Stephen's house church and put him out of business altogether."

Still Stephen refused to give up, convinced that God will never quit loving the Mundanese. With his wife now recovered from her injuries, he is awaiting another God-called pastor to care for his flock so that he can plant another church.

Ordination service in Stephen's country

He rented a house in a subdivision for Mundanese people of lower income and began holding church services in his home. He has worked diligently to create good relationships with the area leaders and has earned the favor of some of them.

The general contractor of the subdivision gave the Church of the Nazarene a plot of land on which to build a church. Even if the Nazarenes could afford to build well, it would not be wise to build a fine building, since that would stir the wrath of people of the majority religion and the church would be targeted for destruction.

Despite the difficulties, Stephen and his fellow laborers won't quit. They know God's plans cannot be frustrated. They have laid hold of God's promises about plans He has for them, plans for a hope-filled future (Jeremiah 29:11).

Stephen—planter of seeds in hard soil—fearlessly faces adversity with his family and people, assured that the Lord of the harvest will give great increase.

4

Julie—Educating "Net Workers" for a Human Harvest

Again, the Kingdom of Heaven is like a fishing net that is thrown into the water and gathers fish of every kind (Matthew 13:47, NLT).

Prevenient grace. This is a cardinal doctrine of the people called Nazarenes. And Julie's path to the Church of the Nazarene and the ministry is a beautiful example of this biblical truth.

Julieta Macainan was the youngest of 12 children in her Filipino family. She attended Roman Catholic schools, including LaSalle College in Bacolod City, where she earned the bachelor of science degree with a management major.

While a sophomore in college, Julie—as she is best known—went to church on a friend's invitation. The people's praying and praise in worship greatly impressed her, and the Holy Spirit put a hunger in her spirit to know Christ personally. *Prevenient grace.* After that experience Julie anguished over becoming so easily upset and her bad language, longing for self-control.

Following college, she worked for an economic development foundation. A Christian coworker's influence made Julie long for something more. Again, *prevenient grace*. Another coworker invited her to a Bible study led by a member of InterVarsity Christian Fellowship. Her experience at the Bible study stirred in Julie an acute hunger for a personal relationship with Jesus Christ. Once again, *prevenient grace*.

At work, Julie's boss made her the assistant general manager. She went by interisland ferry to Manila

Dr. Julieta Macainan Detalo

to obtain further training at the Asian Institute of Management. On board the boat, three Americans—Flora Wilson and her daughters, Elizabeth and Brenda—struck up a conversation with her. They had ferried from Iloilo City to Bacolod to take this larger vessel on its long voyage to the capital. Julie, surprised to hear them speaking Ilongo, welcomed the opportunity to practice her English with them. Flora and her husband, Stanley, were Nazarene missionaries. *Prevenient grace* was active.

The Wilsons' kindness further stimulated Julie's craving to know Christ personally. She calls that providential day the beginning of her conversion. One month later, she boarded the ferry to Manila and, to her delight, she heard Flora Wilson call her name. Again, *prevenient grace.*

During the long voyage this time, Flora talked with her new friend about a personal relationship with Jesus Christ. Julie's hunger, plainly written on her face, was easy for Flora to read. Julie asked more about the Church of the Nazarene and learned that a new church was being planted in her town. When she inquired about its location, she found out it was only one block from her home. She had not known it was there, since she would have expected a magnificent structure rather than a rented storefront. *Prevenient grace* without a doubt.

Upon returning to Bacolod, Julie went to the Nazarene storefront on Wednesday evening to introduce herself to the young pastor, Jerry Tingson, and the other Nazarenes. She told them she'd met Flora Wilson. They welcomed her to the church family, taking her into their hearts, and making her promise to return on Sunday. *Prevenient grace.*

Prevenient grace had become God's saving grace.

She didn't tell her family she'd gone to a Protestant church and would be going back on Sunday, knowing that her mom would admonish her with the words, "Always remember, your brother is a priest."

That Lord's day was another turning point for Julie, like the time on the ferry. Those happy Nazarenes made Julie feel that *she* was the most important person present. Pastor Tingson preached a simple, clear salvation message to about 80 people. The sermon and entire worship service centered on Christ. As soon as the pastor extended an invitation for seekers to come to the altar, Julie went forward along with others. Jesus became her personal Savior that morning, and her heart felt as though it would burst with joy! *Prevenient grace* had become God's saving grace.

For a while Julie tried to keep her new life in Christ a secret from her family, and when the truth did come out, her mother threatened to disinherit her. It was hard to live in a home where the family opposed her commitment to Christ. Often at mealtimes she left the table, rushing to her room in tears.

Yet, rather than separating her from the Lord, the opposition served to make her cling more closely to Him. In her Bible study, Julie was captivated by Christ's words: "The harvest is plentiful, but the workers are few. Ask the Lord of the harvest, therefore, to send out workers into his harvest field" (Luke 10:2). She began to sense God's call to prepare for full-time service. *Prevenient grace.*

When Julie talked with the Wilsons about her call, they encouraged her to study at Visayan Nazarene Bible College (VNBC) in Iloilo City. As soon as she could make arrangements to quit her job, Julie enrolled at the school. *Prevenient grace.*

From her first day on campus, her thirst for knowledge was insatiable. One day in the doctrine of holiness class, Professor Stanley Wilson sensed God's leading to invite the students to completely consecrate their lives to Christ. Julie knelt and presented herself completely to the Lord as a living sacrifice. The Holy Spirit came in fullness, purifying her heart by faith. *Prevenient grace* now became sanctifying grace.

About two months before she was to graduate, Dr. and Mrs. Kenneth Rice from Kansas City conducted a Sunday School workshop at VNBC. Among the many pastors, professors, and students at the seminar, the Rices felt impressed by the Lord to get to know Julie better. They, in turn, offered to help her with advanced studies in the United States. *Prevenient grace.*

In late 1979 Julie traveled to Kansas City to study at Nazarene Theological Seminary, where she stayed in the Rices' home. She also worked in Sunday School Ministries at Nazarene Headquarters, learning much from the directors of women's, singles', and senior adult ministries.

Julie was the first woman educator in the Philippine Church of the Nazarene to earn a doctor's degree.

Upon completing the master's of religious education degree in 1982, she returned to teach at VNBC, her alma mater. Alvin and Bette Orchard, the college directors, asked Julie to serve also as the school's registrar. Denny and Betty Owens, Kyle and Charlotte Green, and David and Elizabeth Browning were teaching at VNBC at that time. The college's staff was actively searching for an ideal place to relocate because of Iloilo's unsafe water, lack of room to expand, and its poor location for serving many major islands of the Philippines.

In 1986 VNBC was relocated to Cebu, second largest city in the Philippines, and its enrollment soared to a record high. One district alone sent 32 students. Julie not only taught and served as registrar but also began work on a doctorate in education. She was the first woman educator in the Philippine Church of the Nazarene to earn a doctor's degree.

One year after the college's relocation, Dr. Julie Macainan became the first national president of VNBC. Other major responsibilities have included several years on the Asia-Pacific Nazarene Theological Seminary (APNTS) Board of Trustees; chairperson for the Philippine National Administrative Board for the Church of the Nazarene; a four-year term as secretary of the Board of the Asia Theological Association, representing over 70 institutions of higher education in 14 nations; and president of the Philippine Association of Bible and Theological Schools for four years.

Julie met and fell in love with Joel Detalo, an APNTS graduate. Joel, who has a rich Nazarene heritage and enormous ministry gifts, is professor of theology and chaplain at VNBC. Julie and Joel's mutual love resulted in a wedding ceremony and lifelong commitment to serve the Lord together in ministry.

The Detalos planted the Mactan Church near Cebu's international airport. Many youths have come to Christ through the Student Keepers Move-

Julie and Joel at their wedding

Julie with Asia-Pacific Region and international Nazarene educators

ment (similar to Promise Keepers, but for high school students in the Philippines) that Joel started.

Today, Dr. Julie Macainan Detalo gives dynamic leadership to VNBC. "Harvested" at sea, she is now training, along with Joel, young adults in the Church of the Nazarene to be "net workers" for a vast human harvest in the Philippines and throughout the Asia-Pacific Region.

5

Timothy— Using Prayer Evangelism to Gather the Harvest

He [Jesus] said to his disciples, "The harvest is so great, but the workers are so few. So pray to the Lord who is in charge of the harvest; ask him to send out more workers for his fields" (Matthew 9:37-38, NLT).

"Yes, Lord," Timothy said, weeping for joy. "Yes, I'll be Your missionary."

Pastor Timothy was leading a dawn prayer meeting at his church, the day after ending a 21-day season of prayer and fasting, when God spoke clearly to him about mission service. Once the decision was final, Timothy's heart was at peace.

Right away he phoned Pastor Jae-soon Lee of Durk Seung Church of the Nazarene to tell him about God's call. A few days before, Pastor Lee had called Timothy and said, "Our congregation is looking for someone to go to the Philippines as a missionary. If you know of someone, let me know."

Now, as the two men visited, Rev. Lee said, "I had hoped *you* would be the missionary."

Rev. Timothy Kim's journey to this juncture had taken an interesting route.

———————

He grew up as Byung-gi Kim in the Korean peninsula's southern sector. His large family felt the strong influence of shamanism—Korea's native animism that involves spirit appeasement and ancestor veneration. Upon graduating from middle school in 1972, he knew he couldn't go on to high school immediately, since his family's finances were limited and most of South Korea's better schools are expensive private institutions.

During the next two years Byung-gi worked at construction and farm labor. Both jobs gave him time to think, and he often thought about his divided, hungry heart. He longed to do right, but his heart would harden and his temper often flared.

When his father found a job in Seoul in 1974, he sent his son to a private high school, unaware that it was a mission school. Before long Byung-gi became interested in the Christian way of life that his teachers taught and lived. When one instructor urged the youth to look for a good church home, he felt both fear and excitement at the prospect. He went to the church next door to his house to ask if he could attend. The people present at that time welcomed him gladly. It was the Nam (South) Seoul Church of the Nazarene.

He and his family began attending regularly.

Their minds and hearts slowly opened to the reality that Jesus is the world's only Savior. They became immersed in the life of the church. Byung-gi acknowledged he was a sinner, expressed genuine sorrow for his sin, and put his trust in Jesus to save him. The joy of the Lord's salvation filled his heart, and it seemed that the whole world had changed.

On Christmas Day 1974, Byung-gi was baptized as a testimony to his new life in Christ and commitment to follow Him. Still, he experienced struggles beyond his ability alone to handle. He learned to call upon the Lord for help. As he heard Pastor Young-baik Kim preach about the work of the Holy Spirit in purifying believers' hearts, he hungered to be cleansed and filled, even though he didn't fully understand it all.

Byung-gi entered Korea Nazarene Theological College (KNTC; now Korea Nazarene University) in 1977 to prepare for future ministry. While the young man attended college, the Holy Spirit came in fullness and gave Byung-gi the inner witness that his heart had been cleansed, his sinful ego crucified with Christ, and his life would be empowered by the Spirit for effective Christian service.

Timothy entered his 21-day fast to receive God's guidance.

Back in Byung-gi's high school years, God had planted in his heart a deep desire to serve Christ, especially as an evangelist. But before attempting to implement any plans of his own, he needed to know *God's* will—both for his next steps and for his long-term future. He began three days of prayer and fasting, a time when he sensed God's call to full-time Christian service. He presented himself as a "living sacrifice" to serve the Lord all his days. There would be no turning back.

Timothy Kim's years at KNTC were a season of growing in Christ, building relationships, and getting to know a beautiful student named Hyun-soon Kang, who later took the name Lydia. They both graduated from KNTC in 1984. His college years had been stretched out, as they are for all Korean young men, for mandatory military service. In February of 1987 Timothy—his Bible name—and Lydia were married.

Timothy and Lydia Kim

That year while serving as youth pastor at the Pung Seung Han Church and working with the Korea Central District NYI, Timothy entered his 21-day fast to receive God's guidance. And that is when God spoke to him about being a missionary.

Timothy and Lydia Kim and their three sons

In March 1988 General Superintendent Jerald D. Johnson ordained Timothy, and Durk Seung Church of the Nazarene commissioned him and Lydia as their missionaries to the Philippines. Later that month the congregation sent them forth as their representatives to the mission field.

The Kims began their service in the Metro

Manila area in the Philippines, making it possible for Timothy to study toward bachelor of theology and master of divinity degrees at Asia-Pacific Nazarene Theological Seminary (APNTS). He studied with others who were called to serve in nations on the four world regions served by APNTS.

Almost five years ago, the field director sent Timothy, Lydia, and their three sons—Yong-Gee, Im-Gee, and Jin-Gee—to Cebu, the second largest city of the Philippines. The mission leader asked Timothy to direct the "Thrust to Cebu City" evangelism effort.

"God, give me the Philippines for Christ or give me death!"

The forces of evil appeared to oppose them. Timothy was hospitalized because he contracted typhoid fever and amoebic dysentery. At one point, his life seemed to be threatened by his illnesses. Additionally, the Kims' oldest son started having frightening nightmares, and their second son was rushed to the hospital with a very high fever. A Korean guest in their home suddenly became ill and had to be hospitalized.

In the midst of such severe trials, Timothy recalled that just before he moved his family to Cebu he'd gone on a 40-day prayer retreat and had fervently prayed, "God, give me the Philippines for Christ or give me death!" During that prayer and fasting time for Timothy, God directed him to mobilize Nazarenes to intercede for the Philippines.

After Timothy's physical recovery, challenges to their work continued. He and Lydia began intensive intercessory prayer and recruited many Filipino Nazarenes to join them. In the following years, God enabled them to see great growth in people's prayer lives. God used Timothy's preaching, leading district pastors' meetings, and coordinating of weekday dawn prayer meetings at Visayan Nazarene Bible College (VNBC) to change pastors, students, and professors.

"Timothy and Lydia have been wonderful to work with, and I have seen significant growth in their understanding of their role on a missionary team," Robert Craft writes. "Timothy is a dedicated, sincere man of God and prayer. His role as a spiritual adviser to the pastors and to *JESUS* film teams is a perfect fit for his gifts."

Through Timothy's influence, preachers, seminar presenters, Youth in Mission and Work and Witness teams have come from Korea to labor in the Philippines. They have fostered a spirit of partnership between themselves and their Filipino Nazarene counterparts, and they also have been enriched by the friendships they have forged.

Korean congregations have helped to provide church buildings and to fund projects at VNBC. Korean pastors have sponsored Philippine National Nazarene Pastors' Conferences, with some of them coming to speak. Their strong emphasis on prayer is helping to bring renewal to the leaders of several districts in the Philippines.

A recent 16-member Korean Youth in Mission

Missionary Timothy Kim preaching in the Philippines

team brought blessing and challenge both to the Korean young people and the Filipino youth with whom they served and to whom they ministered. The team assisted in successful church planting endeavors in three cities—Cebu, Cagayan de Oro, and Iligan.

Timothy is a "man after God's own heart"—an Asian illustration of the power and grace of God to transform a person from fear of evil spirits into a Christian who lives and serves in the fullness of the Holy Spirit. His ministry shows that prayer evangelism is a key to an abundant harvest in the Asia-Pacific Region.

6

Samuel—Training Hands for an Agricultural and Eternal Harvest

Do you think the work of harvesting will not begin until the summer ends four months from now? Look around you! Vast fields are ripening all around us and are ready now for the harvest. The harvesters are paid good wages, and the fruit they harvest is people brought to eternal life. What joy awaits both the planter and the harvester alike! (John 4:35-36, NLT).

One hot, summer afternoon, Jasuh Jana was sitting on the porch of his bamboo house, gazing down the Maekok River. Suddenly the young Red Lahu witch doctor saw striding toward him on the shimmering surface of the river two bearded men dressed in white.

Coming right up to Jasuh, they gazed into his eyes, and one of them announced, "The true and living God will send a messenger to you; heed his message. He will tell you how to know the only true God." They quickly left him.

Soon an evangelist bound for a village downstream stopped to spend the night at Jasuh's village. According to Lahu custom, he looked for the village headman or witch doctor to ask permission to stay overnight. He came to Jasuh, who welcomed him into his home.

After dinner, the evangelist took out a Viewmaster that Samuel Yangmi, Nazarene missionary, had given him. The visitor put in a disc with colored slides, depicting Bible stories. Then he handed the Viewmaster to the witch doctor, showing him how to look through it toward a light source. The first picture that Jasuh saw was from the story of Moses. To the witch doctor's surprise, it showed the two men he'd met in his afternoon vision!

"I've been waiting for you to come with the message of the true and living God!" Jasuh said. "The two men in this picture came and told me to believe your message. How can I know the true and living God?"

The evangelist had never gotten such a reception from a witch doctor. He knew that the Holy Spirit was working, so he changed his plans. Rather than continuing downstream, he stayed to teach Jasuh and his family, bringing them to full faith in Christ. The evangelist began to establish them in Christ and the Word of God, and he sent word for Samuel to come and help them burn all the witch doctor's demon shelves and paraphernalia at the Maekok River bank as a testimony to the other villagers. Jasuh, the witch doctor, was the first Red Lahu to be baptized in northern Thailand.

Sadly, persecution broke out against him and his

Missionary Yangmi working with a Lahu man

family. Villagers began to blame Jasuh for every sickness and problem in the village. They threatened his life if he did not turn his back on Christ and return to witchcraft. Failing to dissuade him, they hired an assassin.

Jasuh Jana and his family fled to a distant village that already had received the gospel. God gave Jasuh's family grace and abiding joy as they began their new lives. Jasuh learned to read and write his own language. Some time afterward, when the local pastor had to be away on Sunday, Jasuh led worship and gave his testimony in place of a sermon. He and his family became mature Christian workers—hands for the eternal harvest.

In the beginning, God had planned that Samuel would work in the Golden Triangle area of Southeast Asia and even in southwestern China. Sam's rescue from death in infancy, his Christian heritage, and his eventual work in the Church of the Nazarene are links in a long chain of heaven-forged preplanning.

Sam's dramatic saga is linked to the story of J. Russell and Gertrude Morse who arrived at Batang, a remote mission station on the eastern border of Tibet, in 1921. Five years later they moved to Yunnan Province in southwestern China. In 1931 they began working among Lisu tribal people, and the following year they adopted two Tibetan Lisu girls who had been orphaned. For two decades they worked in Tibet and Yunnan among the Lisu tribe.

In 1950 the Morses and their adopted daughter Esther Drema moved from Tibet (now a province of China) to the Putao Kachin state in northern Burma (now known as Myanmar). Lisu Christians were fleeing persecution, ethnic cleansing, and famine in China by crossing the snow-covered Himalaya Mountains into Burma. The Morses lovingly labored to help resettle some 20,000 Lisu and Rawang Christians.

In 1954 a Lisu couple sought refuge and medical help for the impending birth of their baby boy. Some time after his birth, Burmese government troops began driving refugees back to China, pushing them out of Burma at rifle and bayonet point.

The couple rushed to the mission station to

hand over their five-month-old son for Esther to adopt. It was likely his sole chance to survive. Esther named him Samuel. Quite a while later she met Jesse Yangmi, a Christian Lisu, and they were married in 1963. Together they reared Sam and served as missionaries alongside the Morses.

The Yangmis, Morses, and a handful of others stayed, surviving by eating monkeys and foraging for food in leech-infested jungles.

In December of 1965 General Ne Win's socialist government ordered all missionaries to leave Burma. Having no other way to get out of Burma, the Yangmis and Morses headed for the border of India, traveling through a forested no-man's-land along with several thousand Lisu Christians. They hoped to find a promised land of peace. Burmese troops pursued them in the dense jungle but failed to capture them because of heavy monsoon rains.

The refugees reached the border of India only to have the Indian authorities refuse to receive them, leaving them stranded in an area that would become known as "Hidden Valley." They suffered severe hardships with little more than the will to survive. Many Lisu Christians returned to China. But the Yangmis, Morses, and a handful of others stayed, surviving by eating monkeys and foraging for food in leech-infested jungles.

They lived in Hidden Valley for six years until 1970, when Jesse, Esther, and Samuel again attempted to enter India. Arrested, they appealed to the authorities not to send them back to Burma for fear of their lives but to allow them to contact Christians in the United States. Permission was granted, and the Yangmis contacted their mission board in the United States. By God's grace and through a special act of the U.S. Congress, the way was cleared for them to go to America.

Jesse took advanced studies at a Bible college to prepare for more effective service among the tribal peoples of the Golden Triangle. While he studied in Joplin, Missouri, Sam attended high school and then began college.

When Jesse completed his training in 1975, he and Esther went to northern Thailand. Sam remained as a sophomore student at Ozark Christian College and began youth ministry in a small rural church in Smithfield, Missouri. Two years later he joined his parents in northern Thailand, where he assisted with a revision of the Lisu Bible and served as a missionary intern in village evangelism.

Sam's heart ached for the plight of so many people who lived in bondage. He began to seek information on a college that offered an agricultural program. He wanted to learn better how to help Lisu and Lahu hill tribal people to break free from the vicious cycle of poverty, dependency on opium cash crops, and addiction to opium. Additionally, Sam began to look to his parents to find a Lahu girl to be his wife in a customary, prearranged marriage.

Sam and Lumae Yangmi with her 94-year-old grandfather, the oldest Lahu Nazarene.

Sam gave his word to his mother he would marry the Christian girl that she and Jesse chose for him.

On November 16, 1978, Lumae Jasai Sairattanyu became Mrs. Samuel Yangmi. Though Sam and Lumae had been in full agreement about the marriage, it was hard for them to communicate—they didn't even speak the same language. They depended heavily on sign language until Sam learned to speak Thai and Lahu.

Those were good days of deepening love for one another, for Christ, and for the people they were serving together. God blessed their marriage, and four daughters were eventually born to them—daughters who would grow up speaking Lahu, Thai, and English.

After some years Sam learned about a program at MidAmerica Nazarene College (now University). Through the help of Charles Morrow, he went to MidAmerica to study in the agrimissions program, accompanied by Lumae and the three daughters they had at that time. Charles's former missionary service in Haiti and his heart for the world profoundly influenced the Yangmis. Sam also had an influence on MidAmerica by helping change the designation of the agrimissions degree to the international agribusiness degree. In fact, he would be the first graduate of that program.

When Morrow and Steve Weber founded Nazarene Compassionate Ministries (NCM) in the early 1980s, Sam Yangmi was there, praying with them about the significant ministries it would make possible.

Many other good things happened for Sam at MANC. Under the teaching of Larry Fine, Sam learned better the biblical doctrine of sin and the doctrine of holiness. As a result, sensing his need for a deeper work of God's grace, he offered himself to God in complete abandonment, and he experienced the cleansing work of God's Spirit. Throughout his time at MANC, the Yangmis felt the friendship and love of Spirit-filled Nazarenes, and they sensed the denomination's heartbeat for world mission.

Following graduation in 1984, Sam and Lumae returned to their work among Thailand's tribal peoples. There was so much to do for God, and they were now better equipped to serve the people. In the ensuing months, the couple saw great growth in the lives of the Lahu hill tribal people they were serving. Through the message of full salvation, coupled with agricultural and compassionate ministries programs that Sam developed, Lahu Christians began achieving self-reliance without succumbing to temptation to grow opium. Villages were transformed, some becoming predominantly Christian.

The Sandell family joined the Yangmis in Thailand. Sandy Sandell had studied at Nazarene Theological Seminary, a fact that served to remind the Yangmis of the Church of the Nazarene. When Sam's sister Lucy was ready to study nursing, he recommended MANC, and she went there. The Sandells' work with the Yangmis and Lucy's study at MANC strengthened the Yangmis' ties to the Church of the Nazarene.

Sam and Lumae, independent missionaries, were lonely. Though supporting local congregations sent funds to help them, it seldom seemed they had genuine interest in them. The Yangmis yearned for a denomination with a firm commitment to fulfill the Great Commission. When the leaders of Nazarene mission work contacted them, Sam and Lumae sensed that they were truly interested in them and their daughters.

In 1988, Robert Scott and George Rench, directors respectively of the World Mission Division and the Asia-Pacific Region, visited Thailand to research the prospects for entering that most Buddhist nation on earth. It was natural for them to contact Sam Yangmi to ask if he knew a way for the Church of the Nazarene to obtain visa "slots" for the Michael

McCartys. How they made contact, however, is little short of a miracle.

Not knowing that Drs. Scott and Rench were in Thailand and trying to contact him, Sam was engaged in village evangelism when the two men arrived in Chiangmai. They had a telephone number for Tom Love, the Yangmis' missionary friend. Tom took the denominational leaders on a long, tiring trip by truck up the rugged mountain terrain to Hueytad village where Sam had been working. When they arrived, they learned that as they were coming up the mountain roads, the Yangmi family had passed them on their way back to Chiangmai.

In the village, Tom introduced the leaders to Lumae's parents who served them tea and told them about Sam's work. They saw directly some of the work he was leading among the tribal people along the Thailand and Myanmar (Burma) border, such as his training of the people in agricultural methods that enabled them to grow tea, coffee, and other cash crops rather than opium.

Sam was also running a program to help free people from addiction to opium. Gary Morsch, a Nazarene physician, had visited their work and given assistance. Steve Weber, NCM director, had also visited the Yangmis during the founding stages of the Maetang Tribal Children's Home, later directing some NCM funds to build a sanitary water system. The tribal children's home allows Lahu, Lisu, and Hmong kids, with no schools in their villages, to be nurtured in a Christian environment close to government-operated schools where they get a sound public education each weekday.

When Drs. Scott and Rench finally got back down from the mountain area to Chiangmai, they contacted the Sandell family, knowing Sandy's association with NTS in Kansas City. That afternoon Sam had felt God's direction to visit the Sandells. Upon arriving at the Sandells' home, he met Bob Scott and George Rench—disappointed to have missed Sam—just as they were leaving for the airport to return to Bangkok. Their meeting was another of God's miracles for the Yangmis and the Church of the Nazarene.

In response to their request for Sam's help to sponsor the Church of the Nazarene to enter Thailand, he and his colleagues worked out an agreement for their independent "umbrella" group to make available to the church some of its missionary visa slots.

Michael (Mike) and Rachel McCarty were transferred from Indonesia to Thailand in April 1989. Dr. Rench asked Mike to serve as director for the Southeast Asia Field. From the beginning of Nazarene work in Thailand, the McCartys and their missionary associates Richard and Jean Knox enjoyed a warm, cooperative relationship with Sam and Lumae.

In time the Yangmis became convinced that their beliefs and Church of the Nazarene teachings were the same. They spoke with the McCartys and Knoxes about giving up their independent missionary status to join forces with the Church of the

Nazarene in Southeast Asia. They appreciated the church's emphasis on the person and work of the Holy Spirit, and the sanctifying grace of God was certainly at work in their lives and ministries.

The McCartys, the Knoxes, the Renches, and other church leaders helped prepare them to join the Church of the Nazarene. After special training and orientation in the States in 1993, the Yangmis received a specialized assignment contract to serve as missionaries with the church in Thailand.

They solved the problem by using large laundry detergent boxes that held much more than the little Alabaster boxes from America!

The Yangmis are giving dynamic leadership to a growing work in scores of tribal villages in northern Thailand. Nazarene medical team members from the Philippines, Japan, Papua New Guinea, and the United States have conducted day clinics and evening evangelistic services there, causing the Church of the Nazarene to be known by many villagers.

Jean Knox tells about the effort Rachel McCarty, Sam Yangmi, and others made to introduce the Alabaster offering concept across the Thailand District. They gave Alabaster boxes to the people to fill with their offerings to purchase land and construct buildings around the world. They coached them to bring their boxes on a designated day. Soon, however, several Lahu congregations complained the boxes were too small. They solved the problem by using large laundry detergent boxes that held much more than the little Alabaster boxes from America!

The Yangmi family

Sam and Lumae now have four lovely teenage daughters—Nellie, Julie, Samantha, and Anzie—two of whom are students at MidAmerica Nazarene University. The Yangmis' ministry includes helping many churches, coordinating several self-help programs, keeping Maetang Tribal Children's Home mission-driven, and providing extension theological education for Lahu and Lisu Christian workers. Independent Lisu Christian congregations have invited Sam to come to their villages in northern Myanmar and southwestern China's Yunnan Province to teach them the gospel as well as the *Manual of the Church of the Nazarene.*

Sam freely crosses into northern Myanmar as few "outsiders" can do, and he returns to the eastern edge of Tibet and western Yunnan to train workers who think of themselves as members of the global Nazarene family. Yunnan is home to 25 of China's 55 major non-Han-Chinese people groups. Han-Chinese people form the dominant group of the nation. Doors keep opening to the church, largely due to Sam's contacts, to work among these minority peoples that China's central government refers to as "nationalities."

From his field of labor in northern Thailand, Sam goes to train workers for the non-Han-Chinese fields in southwestern China. He and a Chinese coworker are training scores of pastors regularly, Sam working with the Lisu pastors and the coworker with Mandarin-speaking pastors. They are partners in developing local Christian leaders to hasten the harvest. In the Lisu Autonomous Region of China, Christians have a significant influence in society. Pre-Christians call Christians the "people who pray." And these praying workers in the Lord's field are obeying Christ's command to "ask the Lord of the harvest . . . to send out workers into his harvest field" (Matthew 9:38).

Even witch doctors and village headmen have come to the Savior.

In the notorious Golden Triangle where most of the world's opium is grown, Sam challenges Satan as he [Sam] helps addicts find deliverance and new life in Christ. The rate of rehabilitation by God's power is beyond that of any government-funded program. Sam also confronts the realm of darkness in dealing with animistic practices of the pre-Christian tribal people.

He dares to declare that Satan's former victims, long held in his clutches but whom Christ has set free, are completely delivered. Even witch doctors and village headmen have come to the Savior through the evangelistic efforts he directs. Sam instructs converts to give bold public testimony to Christ and their resolve to follow Him forever.

When Lahu evangelists and pastors see villagers turn from the power of Satan to faith in Christ, they teach them to overcome their fear of evil spirits. This involves a public ceremony in which they and the converts destroy spirit shelves and paraphernalia from their homes. They take them to the riverside or to the center of the village and burn them.

When Pa Yang village needed a pastor, Sam thought about Jasuh. He went to the former Red Lahu witch doctor and heard Jasuh's amazing testimony in greater detail. Years earlier, when the death sentence had been on Jasuh's head, he had told God if he survived he would give his life in service. God not only had rescued him from the hit man but also had helped him become a Christian leader.

Sam asked him to pray about becoming the pastor at Pa Yang Church. God led him to accept the assignment, and He used Jasuh greatly. In 1994, through the intercession of a visiting team of Korean Nazarenes, revival broke out at Pa Yang village. Families began turning from evil spirits to the Lord God. In October 1994 Jasuh and Sam baptized the village headman and his wife.

Jasuh and his wife came to the first Thailand District Pastors' and Wives' Retreat where Thai and Lahu pastors and their spouses gathered to learn,

Mission leaders in Thailand: (l. to r.) Philip Park, Brent Cobb, Michael McCarty, and Samuel Yangmi.

pray, and worship together. At one point during the retreat, Field Director McCarty asked if anyone had any questions. Jasuh stood with his Bible in hand and said, "Will you teach me how to be a better pastor? I don't have much education, and I don't know a lot about the Bible. But I want to learn to help my people. Will you teach me how to be a better pastor?"

Jasuh's question touched everyone, planting a seed from which sprang the South East Asia Nazarene Bible College (SEANBC). Jasuh had only a fourth-grade education. No commentaries or other sermon helps were available in his language. He only had a Bible, hymnal, and the illumination of the Holy Spirit to help him in his task as a pastor.

Jasuh has now taken every course that has been taught at the SEANBC extension center in Chiangmai, graduating from the course of study for pastors. Jasuh and his entire family attended the Eighth Thailand District Assembly on January 19, 1999. General Superintendent William Prince ordained him and two other Lahu pastors, along with a Thai pastor. Jasuh Jana and his family are exhibits of God's transforming power and grace.

It was a historic district assembly at which the delegates voted to organize into two districts—the Thailand District (serving Thai people) and the Northern Thailand District (serving Lahu and other hill tribal people groups). In the northern Thailand harvest field, Samuel and Lumae Yangmi cultivated the ground and planted good seeds. Eric and Paula Kellerer helped to plant more seeds and to water them. Korean missionaries Philip and Ruth Park helped prepare the harvest. Tomo Hirahara from Japan and his Filipino wife, Ceny, are helping to hasten the harvest.

Vast fields of people groups in northern Myanmar, in China's Lisu Autonomous Region, and in Tibet are pleading for more workers to help sow and water gospel seeds. It is like the impassioned plea the apostle Paul heard during the night: "Come . . . and help us" (Acts 16:9). With heart and soul—drawing on his compassion for unreached peoples and his ability to speak English, Thai, Lisu, Lahu, Kachin, Burmese, and some Mandarin Chinese—Samuel Yangmi is answering that call. And he is sounding the call for others to join in the task of preparing other Asians for the work of the eternal harvest.

Epilogue

The great trumpet will sound, and he will send out his angels to the four corners of the earth, and they will gather his chosen people from one end of the world to the other (Matthew 24:31, TEV).

We introduced the six stories you've just read by noting that many "hands" are needed in Asia's harvest fields to prepare for spiritual planting, plant the seeds well, water the crop, weed or prune, guard against enemies, and join together in the anticipated ultimate task of gathering the harvest with urgency.

- Luz Tamayo, Filipino pastor and trainer of personal evangelists, is seeing God make the dream of a congregation of over 1,000 witnessing Nazarenes become a reality.
- Hitoshi Fukue, motivated by love for the Lord of the harvest, labors tirelessly at Asia-Pacific Nazarene Theological College to train men and women for the Asian and Pacific harvest fields.
- Stephen, resolute in bringing the Redeemer to resistant people in a land that is hostile toward Christians, is still seeing some of the seeds he sows take root and bear fruit.
- Julie Macainan Detalo, having been brought to Christ by caring soul winners and nurtured by patient disciple makers, gladly devotes her life to the task of training more workers.
- Timothy Kim, Korean missionary to the Philip-

pines, ceaselessly sows seeds and waters them with his tears, enhancing the future harvest by his persistent praying and mobilizing people into prayer partnerships.

- Samuel Yangmi, laborer for the Lord in the Golden Triangle of Southeast Asia, is faithfully asking the Lord for more "hands" for the harvest, then putting his own hands and feet to the task of equipping those whom God sends.

Each of these harvest hands knows that the anticipated harvest calls for many hands working tirelessly and cooperatively, but that God alone gives the increase. They are the first to say, "To God goes all the glory for the great Asian harvest."

Pronunciation Guide

The following information is provided to assist in pronouncing some unfamiliar words in this book. The suggested pronunciations, though not always precise, are close approximations of the way the terms are pronounced in English.

Introduction

Lisu	LEE-soo
Rambhau	rahm-BOU
Sahib	sah-HEEB

Chapter 1

Antipolo	an-tee-POH-loh
Aquino	ah-KEE-noh
Bangiad	bahng-GEE-ahd
Baras	BAH-rahs
Bugarin	BOO-gah-reen
Cogeo	koh-GAY-oh
Fernandez	fer-NAHN-dehz
Laguna	lah-GOO-nah
Laurea	LAH-ree-ah
Leongson	lee-OHNG-sohn
Luz Tamayo	LOOZ tah-MAH-yoh
Luzon	loo-ZOHN
Mapua	mah-POO-ah
Morong	moh-ROHNG
Muzon	moo-ZAHN
Norie Mateo	NOHR-ee mah-TAY-oh
Pattee	PAT-TEE
Pidilla	pih-DIH-yah
Sumulong	soo-MOO-lohng
Tanay	tah-NIE
Taytay	TIE-TIE

| Teresa | tuh-RAY-sah |
| Valenzuela | val-ehn-zoo-WAY-lah |

Chapter 2

Airi	ah-EE-ree
Fukue	FOO-kway
Harada	hah-RAH-dah
Hirota	hee-ROH-tah
Hitoshi	hee-TOH-shee
Isewan	ee-SAY-wahn
Kochi	KOH-chee
Makoto Ibuka	mah-KOH-toh ee-BOO-kah
Mitsuko	miht-SOO-koh
Oyamadai	oh-YAH-mah-die
Sano	SAH-noh
Shikoku	shee-KOH-koo
Suzuki	soo-ZOO-kee
Tomoki	toh-MOH-kee
Yoshinoya	yoh-shee-NOH-yah

Chapter 3

| Mundanese | MOON-dah-neez |

Chapter 4

Bacolod	bah-KOH-lohd
Cebu	SEE-boo
Detalo	dee-TAH-loh
Iloilo	EE-loh-EE-loh
Ilongo	ee-LAHNG-goh
Macainan	mah-kah-EE-nahn
Mactan	MAHK-tahn
Tingson	TIHNG-sun
Visayan	vuh-SIE-yahn

Chapter 5

| Byung-gi | BYUHNG-gee |
| Cagayan de Oro | KAH-gah-yahn day OH-roh |

Durk Seung	DUHK SUHNG
Hyun-soon Kang	HYUHN-soon KAHNG
Iligan	ee-LEE-gahn
Jae-soon	JAY-SOON
Nam	NAHM
Pung Seung Han	PUHNG SUHNG HAHN
Young-baik	YUNG-BAK

Chapter 6

Batang	bah-TAHNG
Ceny	SI-nee
Chiangmai	CHANG-mie
Drema	DRAY-mah
Han-Chinese	HAHN chie-NEEZ
Hmong	MOHNG
Hueytad	whay-TAHD
Jasuh Jana	jah-SUH jah-NAH
Kachin	kah-CHIN
Lahu	LAH-hoo
Lumae Jasai	LOO-may jah-SIE
Sairattanyu	sie-rah-TAHN-yoo
Maekok	may-KOHK
Maetang	MAY-TAYNG
Myanmar	MEE-ahn-mah
Ne Win	nee WIHN
Pa Yang	PAH YAHNG
Park	PAHK
Putao Kachin	poo-TAU kah-CHIN
Rawang	rah-WAHNG
Sandell	san-DEHL
Tomo Hirahara	TOH-moh HIH-rah-HAH-rah
Yangmi	YAHNG-mee
Yunnan	yoo-NAHN

Betty Eades 9/8/02

Betty Karnes 10-28-02

Joe Porter 2-12-03